W9-BRP-550

rord, Carin T.
Levi Strauss

5/04

Levi Strauss
The Man Behind Blue Jeans

Carin T. Ford

Enslow Publishers, Inc.

40 Industrial Road	PO Box 38
Box 398	Aldershot
Berkeley Heights, NJ 07922	Hants GU12 6BP
USA	UK

http://www.enslow.com

Copyright © 2004 by Enslow Publishers, Inc.

All rights reserved.

No part of this book may be reproduced by any means without the written permission of the publisher.

Library of Congress Cataloging-in-Publication Data

Ford, Carin T.
    Levi Strauss : the man behind blue jeans / Carin T. Ford. — 1st ed.
        p. cm. — (Famous inventors)
    Summary: Describes the life and career of Levi Strauss, a Bavarian Jew who immigrated to the United States in 1847 and became a very successful businessman and philanthropist after inventing blue jeans.
    Includes index.
    ISBN 0-7660-2249-8
    1. Strauss, Levi, 1829–1902—Juvenile literature. 2. Businesspeople—United States—Biography—Juvenile literature. 3. Levi Strauss and Company—History—Juvenile literature. [1. Strauss, Levi, 1829–1902. 2. Businesspeople. 3. Levi Strauss and Company—History.] I. Title. II. Series.
    HD9940.U4S7927 2004
    338.7'687'092—dc22   2003013726
    [B]

Printed in the United States of America

10 9 8 7 6 5 4 3 2 1

To Our Readers: We have done our best to make sure all Internet Addresses in this book were active and appropriate when we went to press. However, the author and the publisher have no control over and assume no liability for the material available on those Internet sites or on other Web sites they may link to. Any comments or suggestions can be sent by e-mail to comments@enslow.com or to the address on the back cover.

Every effort has been made to locate all copyright holders of material used in this book. If any errors or omissions have occurred, corrections will be made in future editions of this book.

Illustration Credits: © 1999, Artville, LLC, pp. 6, 12; Courtesy of Levi Strauss & Co. Archives, pp. 3, 4, 16, 18, 20, 21, 23, 24, 25, 26, 27, 28; Enslow Publishers, pp. 18 (background), 30; Library of Congress, pp. 7, 11, 14–15; Picture Collection, The Branch Libraries, The New York Public Library, Astor, Lenox and Tilden Foundations, pp. 8, 10; Photo courtesy of Jason Quick, pp. 1, 2, 19.

Cover Illustration: Portrait, patent, and pocket photos Courtesy of Levi Strauss & Co. Archives; leather patch photo courtesy of Jason Quick.

Table of Contents

1 A New Beginning 5

2 From East to West 9

3 Striking Gold 13

4 The Best Pants 17

5 A Good Life 22

Timeline 29

Words to Know 30

Learn More About Levi Strauss 31

Index 32

Levi Strauss was called Loeb when he was a child in Bavaria.

Chapter 1

A New Beginning

Levi Strauss was eighteen years old when he saw America for the first time. It was 1847. He and his family had left their home in Bavaria, a land that is now part of Germany. They wanted to start a new life in America.

The New York harbor was a busy and exciting place. People chattered in different languages. Ships carrying fruits and vegetables, coffee, silk, and sugar

Within the map:

CANADA

Atlantic Ocean

UNITED STATES OF AMERICA

New York

EUROPE

GERMANY

BAVARIA

AFRICA

The trip to New York took many weeks.

came from far-off countries. Sailors and merchants crowded the docks. Boat-builders filled the air with the noise of hammering and sawing.

Levi did not know what America would be like. He surely never imagined that one day his name would be famous throughout this new land.

Levi was born on February 26, 1829, in Buttenheim, a small village in Bavaria. He was the youngest child in the family. His father, Hirsch Strauss, had five children from his first marriage.

Then Hirsch married Rebecca, and they had two more children, Fanny and Levi.

Hirsch was a peddler. He walked from town to town selling cloth, needles, pins, thread, lace, scissors, and other goods. He carried everything in a large, heavy sack on his back. It was hard work.

The Strauss family was Jewish, and they were treated badly in Bavaria. All Jews had to live in one

Ships from around the world docked in New York.

small area, called the Jewish Quarter. There were strict laws about what jobs they could hold and when they could get married.

Two of Levi's brothers—Jonas and Louis—moved to America. They hoped life would be better there. The brothers opened a store in New York City. It was called "J. Strauss Brother & Co."

When Levi was sixteen, his father died of a lung disease. Two years later, Levi sailed across the Atlantic Ocean with his mother and two of his sisters. In New York City, they found Jonas and Louis. Levi's brothers were happy to teach him all about their business.

People came to New York dreaming of better jobs, better homes, and better lives.

Chapter 2

From East to West

evi had very little money. He did not know many words in English. But he was ready to work hard. With his brothers' help, Levi learned about the business of selling dry goods. Dry goods are items like yarn, pins, needles, thread, scissors, combs, buttons, and rolls of cloth. They are the same kinds of things that Levi's father sold as a peddler in Europe.

Levi then went to Kentucky and other parts of the

South for a few years. Nothing is known about what he did during that time. He may have spent his days walking around the country like his father, selling dry goods from a pack on his back. The life of a peddler was not easy. Often peddlers slept outside in a field or in a barn. They washed their socks at night and hung them on a bush to dry.

Peddlers walked along the streets or went door to door.

Levi began to earn money. He also learned how to speak English. In January 1853, Levi became a citizen of the United States. By this time, he was back in New York City. He had a new plan. He would go west to California.

Gold had been discovered in California a few years earlier,

Men put handfuls of dirt into pans, then swished them with water. This was called panning for gold.

in 1848. Thousands of people rushed there with shovels and pans. Their excitement was nicknamed "gold fever." They dreamed that they, too, would find gold and become rich.

But Levi did not want to pan for gold. Instead, he planned to open a dry goods business in San Francisco, California. He would sell his goods to peddlers. Then the peddlers would sell them to men looking for gold.

In the days before trains, some people traveled west

by wagon across the United States. Others went by ship down around the tip of South America and then up to California. Levi took a shorter ocean route. He sailed from New York City to Panama, a country in Central America. Then he and the other travelers

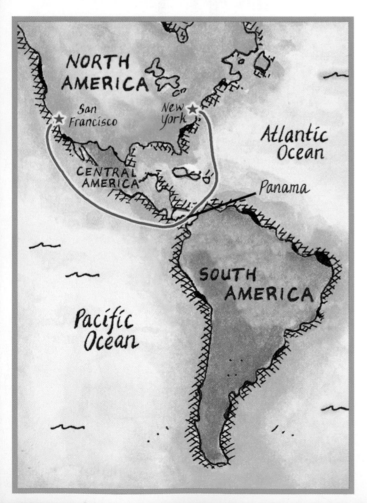

crossed Panama by foot or by mule. From there, they took another boat up to San Francisco. Levi arrived in San Francisco in March 1853.

Levi's sister Fanny also moved to San Francisco with her husband, David Stern. David joined Levi in his business.

Chapter 3

Striking Gold

Levi opened his first business on Sacramento Street in San Francisco. It was near the docks where ships pulled in, loaded with supplies. Levi got most of his goods from his brothers back in New York. But he also needed to buy things from other ships.

San Francisco was a bustling city. People were arriving every day to search for gold. It seemed as if they all needed thread, pins, needles, and blankets.

Levi sold his dry goods to small stores and to peddlers all over the West. The shopkeepers and peddlers who bought their supplies from Levi trusted him as an honest man.

San Francisco was soon crowded with men looking for gold. They set up camps outside the city.

Levi became very successful. He moved into a larger building in 1856.

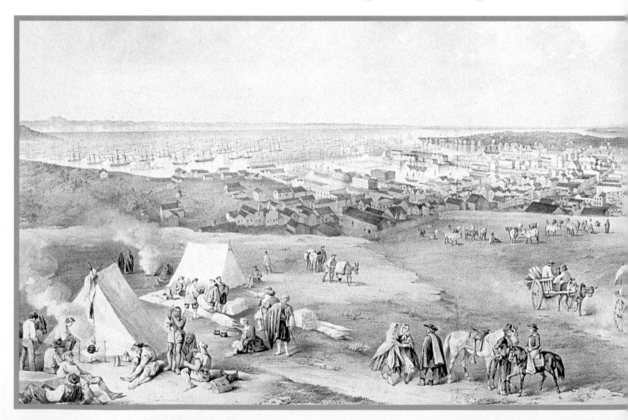

Soon, the name of the business changed from "Levi Strauss" to "Levi Strauss & Co." By 1866 Levi needed even more space and moved his business to Battery Street. At last he had a building that was big enough. Levi's business was also helped by the railroad that stretched across the United States. Trains traveled faster than ships. Levi could now get supplies more quickly from his brothers in New York.

By 1869, railroads traveled from New York to California.

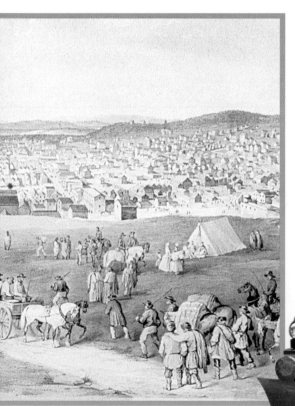

Men like these gold miners shopped in the stores that stocked Levi's goods.

Chapter 4

The Best Pants

In 1872, Levi received a letter from a man named Jacob Davis. Jacob was a tailor in Reno, Nevada. He made work pants from cloth that he bought from Levi's store. He liked to use a heavy cotton cloth or a strong fabric called denim.

One day a woman had asked Jacob to make a very strong pair of pants for her husband. He was a woodcutter, and his pants were always ripping. While

Tailor Jacob Davis had a great idea for making stronger pants.

Jacob was sewing the pants, he suddenly had an idea. He put round pieces of metal, the size of pennies, at the spots that often ripped. These copper pieces were called rivets. Jacob used rivets to make the pockets stronger and to hold them firmly in place.

Jacob's work pants were better than any others. The pockets did not rip off, and the pants did not come apart. People loved these new pants. Soon Jacob was selling many pairs. He did not want other tailors to copy his idea.

rivet

Inventors can protect their ideas with a patent. This is a government paper. It says that the inventor of a new product is the only person who can make it and sell it. A patent lasts for a certain

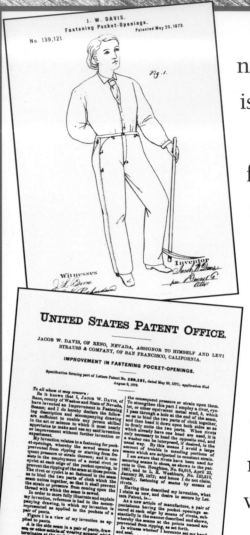

J. W. DAVIS.
Fastening Pocket-Openings.
No. 139,121.   Patented May 20, 1873.

Fig. 1.

Witnesses   Inventor

UNITED STATES PATENT OFFICE.

JACOB W. DAVIS, OF RENO, NEVADA, ASSIGNOR TO HIMSELF AND LEVI STRAUSS & COMPANY, OF SAN FRANCISCO, CALIFORNIA.

IMPROVEMENT IN FASTENING POCKET-OPENINGS.

The patent for Jacob and Levi's riveted clothing lasted for almost twenty years.

number of years. After that, anybody is free to copy the invention.

Jacob needed $68 to apply for a patent. It was a lot of money at that time. So Jacob wrote to Levi. The demand for these pants was "so large that I cannot make them up fast enough," he said. If Levi would pay the fee, Jacob and Levi could get a patent together. Then Levi Strauss and Co. could make and sell these sturdy pants with rivets.

Levi paid the fee, and on May 20, 1873, the government gave Levi Strauss and Jacob Davis a patent. This date is called the "birthday" of blue jeans.

Levi was proud of his company's big building on Battery Street and all his hard workers.

Chapter 5

A Good Life

Jacob Davis moved to San Francisco to work with Levi Strauss. Jacob was in charge of making the clothing with copper rivets. The pants were called "waist overalls" at that time. In Levi's new factory, rows of women worked at sewing machines. They stitched the clothes together and added the rivets.

These waist overalls became popular throughout the west. Miners, cowboys, lumbermen, railroad

22

workers, and farmers asked for them. It was hard for Levi to keep up with all the orders.

Levi wanted to be sure everyone knew that these clothes had come from his factory. So each pair of jeans was marked with a flattened-out **V** shape. It was stitched in orange thread on the back

The dog in this ad is being dragged up the fence because the man's pants do not rip.

pockets. The color matched the orange of the copper rivets. You can still find this stitching on Levi's jeans today.

Here, more than 500 women sew waist overalls in Levi's factory.

LEVI STRAUSS & CO'S
COPPER RIVETED · EVERY PAIR GUARANTEED
OVERALLS
& Spring Bottom Pants

In 1886, Levi's factory started to sew a leather patch to the waist of the jeans. It had a picture of a tug-of-war with two horses trying to pull apart a pair of Levi's jeans. That was to show that Levi's pants were very strong.

Levi Strauss grew very rich. He became an important man in San Francisco. He was a caring man, too, and he used some of his money to help others. He donated money to many charities, such as orphanages and the University of California.

Each pair of Levi's pants has this stitching on the pocket.

Levi went to his office and his factory every day to make sure things were going smoothly. He wanted his factories to be safe. Levi paid his workers well. He did not want the people who worked for him to call him "Mr. Strauss." He asked them to call him "Levi."

One of his workers was Mary Rossi. She was sixteen years old when she worked in Levi's factory.

Levi, seated, was devoted to his brothers and sisters and their children.

"He used to come to the door of the big room where we all worked and look it over," she

said. "He always wore dark suits and carried a tall hat in his hand. . . . He was a nice gentleman."

Levi never married. "My entire life is my business," he once said.

Levi's ads called his clothes "The Two-Horse Brand" to show how strong they were.

"My happiness lies in my . . . work." He was a loving uncle to all his nieces and nephews. When they grew up, many of them worked for Levi Strauss & Co.

Levi died on September 26, 1902. He was seventy-three years old. Levi came to America hoping to make a good life for himself. He became known for his hard work and his honesty. Levi Strauss made clothes that became famous throughout the world. His company still sells clothing to millions of people today.

Levi believed that his company was the most important part of his life.

Timeline

1829~Born in Buttenheim, Bavaria, on February 26.

1847~Arrives in America.

1853~Becomes an American citizen and goes to California.

1866~Moves his business to Battery Street in San Francisco.

1872~Jacob Davis writes to Levi about making denim pants with rivets.

1873~Jacob and Levi get a government patent for their riveted jeans. Levi begins selling jeans, which he calls "waist overalls."

1902~Levi dies on September 26 in San Francisco.

Words to Know

denim—A sturdy cotton cloth. In medieval France, it was called *serge de nimes*. By the 1800s, the English name was shortened to denim.

dry goods—Sewing supplies, cloth, and clothing; not food or tools.

jeans—Denim pants. The word came from *genes*, the name of the pants worn by sailors in Genoa, Italy.

merchant—Someone who buys or sells things.

orphanage—A group home to take care of children without parents.

tailor—Someone who sews clothing.

Learn More

Books

Peterson, Tiffany. *Levi Strauss*. Chicago, Ill.:
   Heinemann Library, 2003.

Roop, Peter and Connie. *California Gold Rush*.
   New York: Scholastic, 2002.

Weidt, Maryann N. *Mr. Blue Jeans: A Story About
   Levi Strauss*. Minneapolis, Minn.: Lerner, 1992.

Internet Addresses

Biography, photos
   <http://www.levistrauss.com/about/history/
   founder.htm>

Inventor of the Week Archive from
   Lemelson-MIT Program
   <http://web.mit.edu/invent/iow/strauss.html>

Index

B
Bavaria, 5, 6, 7–8
Buttenheim,
   Bavaria, 6

C
California gold
   rush, 10–11

D
Davis, Jacob, 17,
   19, 20, 22
denim, 17
dry goods, 9,
   13–14

K
Kentucky, 9

L
Levi Strauss &
   Co., 15, 20, 27

N
New York City,
   5–6, 8, 10, 12, 13

P
Panama, 12
patent, 19–20
peddlers, 7, 10, 14

R
rivets, 19, 22, 23

S
San Francisco,
   California, 11,
   12, 13, 14, 22,
   25
Stern, Davis
   (brother-in-law),
   12
Strauss, Fanny
   (sister), 7, 12
Strauss, Hirsch
   (father), 6–7, 8, 9
Strauss, Jonas
   (brother), 8

Strauss, Levi
   and blue jeans,
      20, 22–23, 25
   becomes U.S.
      citizen, 10
   birth, 6
   childhood, 4, 7–8
   death, 27
   early work, 9,
      10, 11
   growth of
      business,
      13–15
   travels west, 12
Strauss, Louis,
   (brother), 8
Strauss, Rebecca
   (mother), 7, 8

U
University of
   California, 25